Releasing Shame, Guilt and Martyrdom

A guide to Expanding Our Capacity
for Unlimited Goodness

By

Ambika Wauters

Published by
Filament Publishing Ltd
16, Croydon Road, Beddington
Croydon, Surrey CR0 4PA
www.filamentpublishing.com
+44(0)20 8688 2598

To Releasing Shame, Guilt and Martyrdom
ISBN 978-1-913623-84-5
©2022 Ambika Wauters

The right of Ambika Wauters to be recognised as the author of this work has been asserted by her in accordance with the Designs and Copyrights Act 1988 Section 77

All rights reserved
No portion of this work maybe copied in any way without the prior written permission of the publishers

Printed in the UK and USA

What People are saying

As an author, Ambika has given one great insight into the archetypes, energy healing, angels, and homeopathy through her books, writings, teachings, and conversations.

A renown teaching and healer, she has left us wisdom teachings in her gathering of her life experiences and insights.

Many other gifts are in the realm of Life Energy medicine.

Enjoy her through her writings.

My hope is that many more flow from her quill!

TQ

You must get rid of this idea that you are a sinner because it is just an idea that gives you trouble. I don't say that you are a sinner. I know who you really are. You are me, and you are free. The whole world is affected like this. It is in the blood of each generation, and it goes on indefinitely. But it is all imagination. It is a pile of straw that you can destroy with a single match. But you have been so trained to think about sin and good and evil, you even think that setting fire to this pile of straw might also be a sin. It is all these ideas about good and bad, right and wrong, that stop you from striking the match. Your impediments can all go in a bonfire that is lit by a single match. That fire is freedom. Burn everything with this fire of freedom.

HWL Poonja, Sadguru. Teacher and friend

Ambika Wauters

I work as a homeopath, educator, artist, author, healer and product developer. I grew up in southern California, studied history at UCLA, (B.A., class of 1966) and moved to the UK in 1969. I received a Masters in Fine Arts from the Royal College of Art, London in 1972 , I later trained in homeopathy at the School of Homeopathic Medicine, North Yorkshire, UK, receiving a Diploma in Homeopathic Medicine in 1995. I qualified as a member of the prestigious Society of Homeopaths,UK,in 1996.

I have traveled extensively, living abroad for nearly 30 years. I lived in southern Spain for 20 years concurrently with seven years in Zaire, Africa . I enjoyed ten amazingly creative years in the UK; during which time I began my writing career. I have visited India twice, spent three months in Israel writing a book and traveled to Egypt, Morocco, Italy,Greece,Turkey,Russia and Finland . I studied at the C. G. Jung Institute in Zurich, Switzerland, for several months learning the archetypes of the collective unconscious.

Some of my travels were for work, others to learn or teach ; all of it designed to satisfy my restless spirit. I found the world to be beautiful and interesting. It left an indelible mark on me ;teaching me that love unifies people and healing is a universal truth . We all have the innate ability to experience the sacred because it exists within us.

In 1998 I returned to America and in 2001 created the Institute of Life Energy Medicine . This provided an educational base to my work .I began to teach classes on the Human Energy System and offered trainings in homeopathy and the chakras . While continuing to write about energy , homeopathy and healing ,I developed homeopathic products that work on vitality and regeneration and support people through trauma, pain, separation and loss.

I have fifty years of clinical experience working with people in a healing capacity. In the UK I taught homeopathy at Cranfield School of Business Management to business people suffering from the stress of long haul travel . I brought homeopathy into Visa International, Piatkus Publishing and the John Lewis Partnership which operates over 35 businesses. I ran two healing seminars at their castle on Brownsea Island , UK . While in the UK I presented my work on color and sound essences to the Society of Homeopaths . In 2005 I spoke to the College of Syntonic Phototherapy at their annual conference in Kansas City, Kansas, on the healing power of homeopathic color essences.

In 2005 I started The School of Spiritual Homeopathy in Chicago and , later , in Tucson . It ran for five years before I became CEO of the Institute of Life Energy Medicine School of Healing , which is now a completely virtual school, allowing people around the globe to partake of classes, purchase products and benefit from online classes and private consultations. I still contribute to both national and international homeopathic journals sharing my developments in energy medicine and healing .I make my home in Tucson, Arizona. This is where I garden, paint, write and develop remedies.

࿐

This book is available as an audio book. Go to the authors website www.lifeenergymedicine.com

Table of Contents

Introduction: 14

Part One:

Reflections on Releasing Shame, Guilt, and Martyrdom   29

Chapter One : A Dialogue on Shame, Guilt, and Martyrdom   30

Chapter Two :   36

A Practicum: Questions, Meditation, Affirmations, Visualization & Prayer

Chapter Three: 66

Workbook

Part Two:

Pleasure : The Cornerstone of Health   81

Chapter Four: 82

Cultivating Pleasure and Ease

Chapter Five:

Practicum: Questions, Meditation, Affirmations, Visualization, Prayer   104

Chapter Six:

Affirmations   121

Acknowledgments

This book has taken many years to complete. It came out of a desire to heal martyrdom, both my own, and the collective martyrdom in the world. My experiences, both personal and as a professional, have shown me how martyrdom corrupts growth and diminishes healing.

There have been many people throughout my life who helped me heal and transform my fears and negativity. I come by martyrdom naturally and just accepted it as part of my cultural inheritance.

Born into an American Jewish family at the end of World War 2 there was always fear lurking in our family. Memories of the Holocaust kindled the threat of antisemitism in our community and country.

Later in life the Women's Movement made it clear women had been belittled and dismissed from the time of Eve. It was definitely time to claim responsibility for our lives and own our power.

As a mature woman of a certain age I found martyrdom rampant in the lives of the elderly, who were all too willing to give up and give in. They were unwilling and, at times, unable to fight the good fight.

Martyrdom was something I had to face in order to develop health and well being and age with grace and beauty.

I wish to thank the following people for giving me a hand up when I needed it and whose consciousness and kindness took me to higher ground. They are shining lights, examples of kindness, clarity and vision and I am deeply grateful they came for a "reason or a season" , as publisher Chris Day said to me in a recent conversation.

To my Israeli friends, who I met during my two and a half months in Jerusalem and Safed in winter/ 2010:

Audrey Benaroche, a brave, strong, young woman, who taught me kick-boxing when I was 65years old . She strengthened me and brought out the fire and grit to fight the good fight, within and without.

To Karen Pichel, a very bright light in a really dark place ; To Mark Nissack, a remarkable healer and teacher who initiated me into mystical Judaism in the holy town of Safed.

Thank You all for your light, love and, especially, your courage. It helped transform me from a martyr to a warrior.

To the many healers who helped ignite my creative passion and release lifetimes of anger and grief that blocked my ascent to higher planes of consciousness. You have my thanks.

A special gratitude to a remarkable soul, Nina Admiral, who has helped me grow in love, integrity and truth for 20 years. I love you.

To my dear friend: Gaynor Gabriel, who took me by the hand , literally, and helped me move forward .You have been a friend and mentor for the last 30+ years; in love and gratitude.

To Susan Mears, friend and literary agent .You have watched my back and been of true service taking my books to the world. Bless you .

To Tony Mazza, Sr, partner, companion and friend: you bless me with laughter, delight and great cuisine every blessed day we share together. Thank you .

To Chris Day , publisher of Filament Books; an innovative, disciplined thinker who has redesigned publishing and who honors authors. Be blessed in all your efforts.

To students at Life Energy Medicine School of Healing ,I offer you the best I have for loving, understanding and healing people, animals and nature.

I am delighted when you run with the work and make it yours.

To my beloved spiritual teacher, HLW Poonja, better known as Papajii , whose wisdom and guidance allowed me to fundamentally transform the way I engage with life . OM SHANTI OM.

To my sister, Nita Steinberg, blessings of love and health.

Introduction:
a poem by Charlie Chaplin

As I began to love myself

I found that anguish and emotional suffering

are only warning signs that I was living

against my own truth.

Today, I know, this is Authenticity.

As I began to love myself

I understood how much it can offend somebody if I try to force my desires on this person, even though I knew the time was not right and the person was not ready for it, and even though this person was me.

Today I call this Respect.

As I began to love myself

I stopped craving for a different life,

and I could see that everything

that surrounded me

was inviting me to grow.

Today I call this Maturity.

As I began to love myself

I understood that at any circumstance,

I am in the right place at the right time,

and everything happens at the exactly right moment. So I could be calm.

Today I call this Self-Confidence.

As I began to love myself

I quit stealing my own time,

and I stopped designing huge projects

for the future. Today, I only do what brings me joy and happiness,

things I love to do and that make my heart cheer, and I do them in my own way

and in my own rhythm.

Today I call this Simplicity.

As I began to love myself

I freed myself of anything

that is no good for my health –

food, people, things, situations,

and everything that drew me down

and away from myself.

At first I called this attitude a healthy egoism.

Today I know it is Love of Oneself.

As I began to love myself

I quit trying to always be right,

and ever since

I was wrong less of the time.

Today I discovered that is Modesty.

As I began to love myself

I refused to go on living in the past

and worrying about the future.

Now, I only live for the moment,

where everything is happening.

Today I live each day,

day by day,

and I call it Fulfillment.

As I began to love myself

I recognized

that my mind can disturb me

and it can make me sick.

But as I connected it to my heart,

my mind became a valuable ally.

Today I call this connection Wisdom of the Heart.

We no longer need to fear arguments,

confrontations or any kind of problems

with ourselves or others.

Even stars collide,

and out of their crashing, new worlds are born.

Today I know: This is Life!

THE DIVINE HEALS ALL

I forgive and release the toxic past

I ask God to take it from me,

Clear out infections on all levels of being,

All fear of failure,

All lack of self worth,

All ambivalence about life,

All anger and resentment,

All rage and fury.

I choose love, peace and joy

Fully , now.

A prayer by

Ambika Wauters

The premise of this book is to identify shame, guilt and martyrdom that make us renounce our birthright to a good life . What makes us fall into the dark and bottomless pit that is a terrible burden to our spirit and weighs us down in the mire of negativity? Shame is heavy, guilt pulls us down and martyrdom snuffs the oxygen out of the air we breathe.

This book is a guide to restore vibrancy and balance . It works with positive ideas, healing meditations, visualizations, affirmations and non denominational prayers. All take you onto higher ground.

The book encourages spiritual development and to cultivate a higher consciousness. You want to make choices that are compatible with your highest consciousness; choices that will expand your capacity for pleasure and ease.

Each step you take towards healing transforms your ability to create the life you want. Hopefully, you will choose a good life where you thrive, prosper, and flourish.

You want a life that honors your gifts and talents, as well as your ability to love and be loved and build a life that sees you healthy, wealthy and creative.

By releasing your sense of scarcity and lack as well as feelings of deprivation ,you open a channel for good to flow into your life. As you let go of the need to punish yourself and blame others you release shame, guilt and martyrdom.

Martyrdom is defined as the inability to experience pleasure and joy. It negates a belief in happiness and denies you pleasure.

Martyrdom re-enforces punishment and pain. It locks you into feeling entitled to self pity and deepens your sense of worthlessness. It is rooted in familial, institutional and religious expectations to be perfect. It carries an underlying belief that sacrifice, impoverishment and loss is good .

Martyrdom focuses on making you overly responsible for the welfare of others. Your well being is seldom part of the equation of the choices you make ; they generally revolve around pleasing others.

Martyrdom is the crucible in which guilt and shame take root. They make us feel ill, unworthy and frightened.

You may have some " AHA!" moments as you read through this book in which you recognize old familiar patterns. You may have memories that shame you and make you feel something is wrong with you.

If you can put your thoughts aside long enough to read this book you may be willing to move past these unhealthy archetypes and chose to build a new foundation where you see yourself as strong, capable, lovable and worthy of what you say you want. You decide its time to stop undermining your self worth and destroying your self confidence .

Once you can identify the negative patterns that have held you back you can make the decision to expunge shame and guilt from your life . You give yourself permission to let go of negative beliefs and allow the good to flow in now.

The keys you will work with in this book are:

FORGIVENESS, SELF LOVE and PLEASURE.

These are the tools that assist you in releasing self hatred, self abuse and harsh punishment and that lead to martyrdom. They help you claim your power to stop addiction to pleasing others. You create a strong foundation of self worth, self respect as well as a benevolent self love.

We all have a choice to release the beast in us as well as the neurotic need to be perfect. In letting go you open your spirit to receive the good. The choice is yours.

If you want a dreary, gray ,unloving existence you will manifest it. If you want a life rich in grace and joy it is open for the asking. You always have to choose.

If you choose the path of pleasure and ease your life will be full of endless opportunities for gratitude. You become thankful for who you are, what you have, and what you do. You accept your experiences as part of your life and you learn to trust in the good.

A universal principle is this : the universe only knows how to say yes . When you say you are ugly and no one loves you the universe will say YES.

If you affirm you are beautiful and everyone loves you the universe will say YES,

The choice is yours. What will it be? Its up to you!

Some extra pointers in the direction of healing:

Goodness:

Goodness is divine energy that flows to us as we align ourselves with our highest good. Francis Scoville Shinn, healer and author from the 1930's, said goodness was the Divine Design working in our lives as : HEALTH, WEALTH, LOVE AND PERFECT SELF EXPRESSION.

By creating a firm foundation for goodness to find you affirm your worth and honor your choices for love.

When you say " YES" to what you love you invite the good to unfold. You call it into your field. One favorite affirmation from Francis Scoville Shin is :

"NOTHING IS TOO GOOD FOR ME. NOTHING IS TOO WONDERFUL TO HAPPEN OR TOO GOOD TO LAST. "

This affirmation deserves constant repetition. Let it be a reminder you are always worthy of what you say you want, ALWAYS!

This affirmation destroys negativity. It gives you permission to harvest out unworthiness, self loathing and self disgust. It gives you permission to call in the good and to feel blessed about your life.

Forgiveness:

Forgiveness releases the hold guilt, shame and martyrdom have on your soul. It brings peace of mind and cleanses the toxicity your negative thoughts create.

If you want a place at the table of the Great Feast of Life you are asked to leave pain, trauma, disappointment, and loss behind. Forgiveness is the way you get an invitation to that party.

Allow your affirmations to resonate with the good you seek. Take responsibility for what you want and invite it into your life. Claim your good now. It is waiting in the ethers of your consciousness to manifest at this very moment.

When you believe you are worthy of everything you say you want the past is released. If you feel entitled to hold onto your anger you are only feeding your ego, not your spirit. Let it go.

If you refuse to forgive and choose hatred you are only poisoning yourself. If you prefer drama, anger and grief over freedom, joy and peace you will suffer. The choice is yours.

Affirmation:

I RELEASE MY LACK AND SCARCITY CONSCIOUSNESS AND TRUST THE GOOD.

The choice to thrive, enjoy life and find pleasure is yours alone. You must decide you are worth it. Goodness takes many forms. It is delight, laughter ,happiness, reward , opportunities , fun, joy , and healing . All this is yours for the taking . Holding on to your negativity is only a cover up for your feelings of unworthiness.

Give yourself permission to flourish and thrive. Your thoughts have power so let go of a belief , an expectation or a desire for punishment. It is not part of your soul's evolution. We are a culture that loves to punish. We have forgotten about grace and mercy.

Affirmation: I RELEASE AND LET GO OF THE EXPECTATION , FEAR AND BELIEF IN PUNISHMENT.

Affirmation:

I LET GO OF A BELIEF IN PUNISHMENT. IT IS NOT PART OF MY SOUL EVOLUTION.

This Book:

This book cultivates self love, confidence and trust. It helps develop a deeper sense of personal identity and nurtures a belief in your self worth. It affirms your right to the life you say you want.

The book assists you in honoring your self, valuing what you have , and respecting what you do. It opens a window of opportunity for you to be happy and enjoy your life.

No matter how awkward, uncomfortable or irritating things are right now the way up and out of suffering is through forgiveness and gratitude.

Learn to bless yourself, bless your life and the people and things in it. Move forward in the best way you can and give thanks . Your life is so precious; stop taking it for granted.

As you develop clearer intentions for receiving your good you will manifest the life you desire. Let go and open the channels for healing . When you do your higher purpose comes into focus. You develop clarity and know what choices to make for your dreams to manifest in reality.

When you love yourself and do good you make your patch of the universe a better place. One day your awareness of the miracle of life will become your prayer of thanks. The dark moments will fade away and become the cornerstones for your healing, development and maturity.

Affirmation:

GOD IS MY ENDLESS SUPPLY FOR EVERYTHING I WANT AND DESIRE . EVERYTHING COMES TO ME EASILY AND QUICKLY, UNDER GRACE AND IN PERFECT WAYS.

Pleasure and Gratitude:

As you heal you ll realize goodness wants to be shared. It makes you kinder, more compassionate and more pleasant to be around. Pleasure pumps endorphins , releasing Oxytocin, the happiness hormone, into your bloodstream . It purifies every cell in your body and keeps you buoyant, healthy and happy. Enjoy the good . It is a blessing. It places the center of power within you and connects you with the Divine .

Affirmation:

I GIVE THANKS FOR THE PLEASURE AND EASE I EXPERIENCE. I AM OPEN TO RECEIVING EVERYTHING I COULD EVER WANT AND NEED.

Part One

Reflections: Releasing Guilt, Shame and Martyrdom

Chapter One

A Dialogue on Shame, Guilt, and Martyrdom

Doctors have identified a new condition called Pleasure Deficit Disorder. This is a condition defined as people being unable to enjoy themselves. They avoid pleasure, not wanting to engage with anything where feeling is involved. They have a "why bother" attitude that keeps them numb, disconnected and unable to experience their emotions.

Whole cultures , known in the past as able , fun loving people , capable of a good time, able to relax and partake in joy, have lost an interest in pleasure and ease .

People are consumed by the need to make money and get ahead. They end their working day exhausted, too tired to do things they used to enjoy. Their lives have become tedious, their enjoyment level is at an all time low.

Holland, once regarded as a sexually liberated country, now has to show sex education films on TV after 8PM to adults. Their birthrate is down and they are simply not interested in pleasure pursuits.

People are worried about their survival; they fear war, economic downturn, refugees and immigrants, losing their jobs and are terrified their children will not cope in the digital age. Anxiety levels run high.

People seek medication to assuage their fears even at the cost of weight gain and losing their sex drive. Their connection with ease and pleasure is at the bottom of the "to do" list.

Depression runs rampant in western countries today. So many people are on anti-depressants; plumped up on sedatives, cosseted with medication to move their bowels, control diarrhea , manage blood pressure; the litany of conditions runs for miles and it is growing daily.

These medications, while managing stress , make people fat, lethargic and uninterested in pleasure.

They lose their sex drive, over eat carbs to soothe their acidic intestinal track. They have forgotten to connect with their Creator in their hour of need and their trust in life is shrinking into non existence. They need help to get through these challenging times.

People on medications have forfeited their right to happiness, while keeping their minds numbed from having to feel. They live in a gray, neutral zone, where they are unresponsive and detached.

Their children and their pets are also on medications for ADD, ADHD and other psychological conditions. The young are experiencing insecurities they inherited from their parents and they are prone to high anxiety . Worse is they think medication is a way forward rather than tapping into their innate resources. "Better living through chemistry " is a serious delusion.

People experience acute fears and are uncertain about life. They lack confidence in their ability to cope. Kids are now pushed to achieve, make high marks, go to the " best" schools. Very few have developed imaginations, or even enjoyed their childhood. There is a lack of personal identity. They want to look like the latest film star, or they want precocious sex to act like they are more sophisticated than they actually are.

They live disconnected from their emotions and disassociated from nature . They are joyless, careless and prone to accidents because they are detached from their sensation function which connects their instincts to their intelligence and spirit.

Even pets, who live in the astral forces of their owners, are prescribed anti-depressants for their hard to manage and challenging behavior.

We have a problem here. If we believe in "better living through chemistry" we are delusional about what these medications do. Most people are ignorant of what they are putting into their bodies and how these drugs affect their emotional and spiritual lives a well as their physical pathology.

Suppression means never having to deal with emotions, or revealing our sadness, self pity, or rage at not being seen or understood.

With a failure to trust life we see people fall into paranoia and suspicion. Where there is a lack of spiritual values we see people feel it is alright to lie, take what they feel entitled to without considering others. What connects people to a higher power is their belief in life , a trust in the good and an indelible connection to the Divine.

We have weakened our spirits and find it a challenge to step up to higher ground. We have drained our supply of adrenalin which is reflected in the high incidence of chronic fatigue, ME and other auto immune conditions.

Few understand that relaxation, ease and pleasure are nature's true medicine. Homeopathy , acupuncture and herbalism are medicines compatible with your higher consciousness. They help people develop and grow as well as heal.

True healing comes when you look within and release what no longer serves your development or highest good. When you can determine what your personal wounds are you see what needs to be healed. If you fail to develop your own inner resources you become a slave to the external props of healing; you will suck the oxygen out of the room trying to get the energy you need. Chemicals, vaccinations, medications, recreational drugs all challenge your body to break down and assimilate, while suffering and have long term side effect.

Make a choice. When you give power to medications to transform the way you live you dis-empower yourself. You become a pawn of Big Pharma and the dictates of the medical profession to tell you how you are.

Shame and guilt will affect the way you go forward in life. They influence your ability to make wholesome choices for your highest good. They blind you to how you can flourish using your God given talents and trained skills to do well and thrive.

If you are willing to explore the nature of shame and guilt you can release it, you can free your spirit to soar and achieve what you long for and desire. You open the doors to happiness, joy and fulfillment when you allow your light to shine.

If you hold onto negativity it will be challenging to create the life you want. Your relationships will be based on your need to cover up shame and guilt, you will try to prove you are something other than who you are.

Instead of relaxing you ll be hyper vigilant about covering up your desperation.

You will draw friends, colleagues , mentors and bosses who will feel the weak link in your armor and can easily exploit your diminished sense of personal identity and low self worth.

Once you are willing to examine the situations, people and events that contributed to your shame and guilt you ll have a handle on how you limit your life . You ll soon be able to move past it. It takes time to revive the memories and understand the emotional dynamics that created our world view.It is , however, well worth an investment in time and energy to do so.

There is no end to human suffering. Being victimized has a short " feel good" factor. It is always healthier to become the warrior rather than the victim. Being a warrior honors the spirit of who you really are.

It is up to you to take responsibility for your life and choose your path. That includes honoring your wounds and finding viable solutions that allow you to heal. Be grateful and find blessings in everything you do . It will empower and strengthen you.

Part One: Chapter Two

A Practicum: Questions, Meditation, Affirmations, Visualization &Prayer

This chapter offers a practical approach to addressing shame, guilt and martyrdom. Releasing these requires self inquiry; and a willingness to look within . When we examine our attitudes and reflect on painful experiences with love, compassion and understanding we initiate the healing process.

This is an inside job that requires both intention and detachment as it means releasing your addiction to suffering. Results are dependent on you letting go of the underlying belief that you are not good enough and unworthy.

The question here is : do you want empowerment or victimhood? If you desire happiness, well being , prosperity and love consider these exercises. They put you on the path of a lifetime journey that strengthens self love , healing and personal growth.

Work with the following questions and study your responses to them. What comes up for you when you examine the following questions? How do they make you feel? What do they evoke?

Observe your thoughts, watch your behavior. Use the workbook to write your thoughts, feelings and answers to these questions. Refer back to your answers in a few months and notice if there are changes in the way you feel. This is a way of knowing that the changes you have been working on have been effective.

Questions:

1. Do you surround yourself with good, loving people who support you?

_____
_____
_____
_____
_____

2. Do you honor yourself first? If not, then why not?

_____
_____
_____
_____
_____

3. Are you afraid you will lose your relationships, your job, your edge with people if you take care of yourself first? How does that make you feel?

_____
_____
_____
_____
_____
_____

4. Do you put up with bad behavior and insults from people? Why would you take that on? How does that make you feel?

_____
_____
_____
_____
_____
_____
_____-

5. Do you allow people to diminishes or dismiss you? Who are the people who are abusive to you? How does that make you feel?

_____
_____
_____
_____
_____
_____-

6. Are you aware accepting insults and putting up with bad behavior allows others to control you? How do you feel about being controlled and manipulated?

_____
_____
_____
_____
_____-

7. Are you self effacing? Are you timid and shy? Can you set a boundary and stand up for yourself?

_____
_____
_____
_____
_____

8. Do you allow yourself to receive love, kindness, care and respect? Can you take a compliment? Can you validate yourself? Your efforts?

_____
_____
_____
_____
_____

9. In examining the answers to these questions how would you evaluate your level of self respect? Self love? Self care? Use a scale of 1 to 10, 10 being the highest? How do you feel about your answers to these questions?

_____
_____
_____
_____
_____
_____
_____-

10. Can you accept there are no victims in the process of self healing? Would you be willing to give up the victim role? How do you feel when you perceive yourself as a victim? Can you change that dynamic quickly and effectively?

_____
_____
_____
_____
_____
_____-

11. Are you willing to be responsible for your life? Can you honor your choices, be clear about your intentions and allow yourself to claim what you truly want and trust you will receive it?

_____
_____
_____

12. Can you allow the gift of forgiveness to bless you as well as those who have hurt you?

13. How do you feel when you see others hurt, abused or manipulated? Do you ignore it? Try to help? Can you remain objective, if possible?

14. Do you believe you can have what you claim you want?

15. Why do you allow negative thoughts to rule your life? Are you willing to start affirming your worth and honoring your choices for love?

_____
_____
_____
_____
_____

16. Do you feel you are good enough for what you say you want?

_____
_____
_____
_____
_____
_____

Answer these questions in the most truthful way you can. Be prepared for memories to surface and images to show themselves in your mind's eye. You may feel like crying , feel sorry for yourself, feel anger and desire revenge when the memories surface.

You may be reminded you were hurt or treated unkindly . Take time with each person, each memory and begin forgiving now. Take on only what you want to deal with now.

Write their names and situations down in the workbook so you can remember who needs forgiving . You may need to release people several time over months, even years, for the way they treated you. Forgiving is not embracing these people ; it is merely letting go and releasing them from your memory bank. Forgive, release, let go, be free. Amen.

Here are two useful affirmations to use for forgiveness. They were given to me by , Nina Admiral, and I have found them beneficial and effective:

" I FORGIVE YOU, AND RELEASE YOU WITH GOODWILL AND BLESSINGS"

I FORGIVE YOU FOR WHO YOU ARE AND RELEASE YOU TO LIVE YOUR LIFE".

Reflect:

Be willing to see how victimized you have been. Try to understand how you allowed yourself to be belittled, bullied, diminished, dismissed and abused. Once you recognize the patterns its time to move on.

Write your responses down in the workbook. From time to time see if you still feel anger and rage about the way you were treated. You will know you are healing when your response is indifference and your anger neutralized.

If you blame others for your pain you are not taking responsibility for yourself. You can never grow up until you become responsible, even for the worst case scenarios. Just own your part in the incidents. It is never a one way situation.

Forgiveness does not mean you have to like or love your adversaries. You forgive and let go of the attachment to them. Move on to higher ground. Leave the perpetrators to their own lives. When you forgive and let go your whole energy field begins to radiate light, love and goodness and that which you want and desire begins to flow to you.

This is not about culpability for the experience you suffered, nor is it about punishment. It is about letting go so you can be free. This requires consciousness, reflection and the ability to forgive and release your anger and hurt. This is how you become free.

1. Can you love and cherish yourself?
_____
_____
_____
_____
_____-

2. Do you know you are worthy of kindness, love and respect?

_____
_____
_____
_____
_____

Forgiveness requires courage, and a willingness to let go and move on. Try it! It will set you free.

Shame is the feeling you have done something wrong; and that you are fundamentally not right in some way.

3. Do you believe you are fundamentally bad and intrinsically unworthy? Are you willing to rethink this attitude?

_____
_____
_____

4. Do you feel, at some level, you do not measure up?

_____
_____
_____
_____

The addiction to self loathing can only be transformed and released through self love; by embracing who you are and forgiving yourself for the past are you able to live in the moment in peace, love and joy.

Begin by forgiving yourself for believing that what was done to you is your fault.

5. How do you feel about this?

_____
_____
_____
_____
_____
_____

Forgive others for what they said or did to create your thoughts of unworthiness.

6. How do you feel when you forgive the past?

_____
_____
_____
_____
_____
_____
_____

Shame and guilt are reflected in the ways you treat yourself.

7. How do you punish and deprive yourself?

_____
_____
_____
_____
_____
_____

8. Do you feel your anger is justified? Does it make you feel better? Does it lock you into an adversarial position with this person or situation?

_____
_____
_____
_____
_____
_____-

9. Do you avoid seeing just how cruel and mean others were to you?

_____
_____
_____
_____
_____
_____-

10. How do you feel about the way you were treated?

_____
_____
_____

_____
_____
_____
_____

11. Can you acknowledge your feelings and let them go?
_____
_____
_____
_____
_____-

12. What are you willing to do to transform the feeling that you are not worthy of what you say you want?
_____
_____
_____
_____
_____
_____-

13. Are you willing to affirm you are worthy of love, kindness and respect?
_____
_____
_____
_____
_____-

Write your responses in the workbook and refer to it in a few weeks to see if there is still a charge of self hatred or anger associated with this situation or the people involved.

It is a rigorous , highly disciplined training to be kind, forgiving and loving to yourself in any situation where you feel challenged and are made to feel wrong. When you love yourself and you have forgiven you are free of entanglements , free of perpetrators and you will find others who are capable of loving you and value you for who you are.

I AM WORTHY IN THE EYES OF GOD.

This is a beautiful affirmation that takes others out of the equation . It affirms you at a soul level. If you punish yourself for failing in life you ll never win. Learn to love yourself unconditionally through the highs and lows. Love yourself as the Divine loves you.

Otherwise you will become a martyr ; full of self pity and blaming others who have been abusive. Shame and guilt survive on the false platform that you are not good enough. When you fail to own your power because you don't feel worthy you wind up empowering those who have hurt you.

If you choose to believe the negativity others projected on you than you will be miserable; then you will feel unworthy of kindness, love and respect. You will identify yourself as bad, ugly, and dirty; and never be good enough for yourself .

It takes courage to start healing . It takes love to fill your heart cavity with warmth, truth and kindness for yourself. You are being asked to give up every negative idea about yourself you ever felt. You are being asked to love who you are and honor what you want for yourself.

Your job is to be kind to yourself whether you make a mistake, have an error of judgment or when you disappoint someone for not being perfect. That is how you transform shame and guilt into love and kindness. Love is the healing factor that frees you. You become your own good mother and learn to love yourself .

When you allow shame and guilt to rule the choices you make you never win. You can't win when you believe you are unworthy, because shame and guilt will weigh heavily on our heart.

When you are addicted to your own negative self image you live with a constant sense of lack and deprivation. If you feel you are not good enough nothing you do or have will ever be right either. This hardens you as you close off to the divine within you.

When lack of self worth runs your behavior your actions will be less than stellar. It opens the doors for despair and hopelessness and becomes the bottomless pit of martyrdom. Your negative attitudes create illness that blocks you from receiving good.

You can easily become addicted to misery when these negative thoughts get stirred up. They make you feel your anger is justified, and that you are entitled to more than you receive. Your addiction to unworthiness keeps you feeling victimized . This is the attitude that needs changing.

The real issue you face is that you have come to believe and accept your unworthiness as the truth rather than a sick and unwholesome thought about yourself. If you fail to develop a healthy perspective and detachment from your negativity your attitudes will ruin your life.

You connect with your own true nature as you release shame , guilt and martyrdom. As you become aware of these patterns energy begins to flow into your body, healing wounds , repairing perceptions and allowing you freedom to be your optimal self.

Try not to get hooked into believing you are or were wrong. It is simply a thought that you need to change. Loving yourself is the be all and end all of healing, not to mention falling in love with life.

The world is a reflection of your inner state and shame and guilt are nothing more than creations of your own mind. Horrific as they can be, they are still just illusions that you are attached to and believe to be true rather than an idea that simply blocks your joy.

Stop believing what others tell you or imply . Begin to make your own choices. Know who you are and what you can or can not do. Define yourself as a strong person, able to love , appreciate beauty , and emotionally capable of kindness and mercy. Smile at yourself and know you are worthy. Learn to laugh and see the humor in things. For some this is a daily practice. Remind yourself of your worth in a world where people are determined to control your thoughts, and diminish you for their power. Self love connects you to Source and Source is love, joy, truth, and wise guidance.

Be willing to hear angels whisper in your ears, guiding you to connect with good people, enjoy meaningful and rich experiences and find peace of mind. That is what the spirit realm seeks for those who give up self hatred, small mindedness and lack of self esteem.

The real truth about being filled with shame and guilt is that it makes you vulnerable to exploitation and manipulation. You become prey for those who know how to exploit weakness with flattery, charm and cunning. This is how people take away your power and diminish you and leave you feeling small. Know the psychopathic qualities charmers have . They can build you up and tear you down , especially when you try to stand up to them. Be a warrior. Love truth and value it. Stand tall!

Wisdom is realizing you are far more than you can imagine yourself to be or how others perceive you. Yes, people can be cruel , and life can be unfair and you can be disadvantaged. So what? Keep moving forward , be kind in spite of others, embrace the good and value life.

Only you have the power to accept what life has given you in gratitude and to know what your talents and gifts are. They were gifted to you for a reason and that was to do good with them. Find out what you love doing, what you're good at and begin to develop skills that allow you to be your best.

You have a choice to receive the good and bless it and be grateful . Build a strong foundation of self worth and release the demons of self loathing and unworthiness that stand in your way. You are powerful standing on your own, assessing your worth and dismissing what others have to say. Make a clear decision: do you capitulate to negativity or choose the light?

More Reflective Questions: Use your workbook pages to write your answers as well as memories from the past that creates a sense of worthlessness or lack in you.

Self Worth:

1. How well do you love and value yourself?

_____
_____
_____
_____

2. Do you have a sense of how good you truly are or do you despise yourself?

_____
_____
_____
_____
_____-

3. Are you dependent upon other people's opinions of you to know your worth?

_____
_____
_____
_____
_____

4. Do you play yourself down to avoid anger, jealousy and wrath from others? Do you hide your light under a bushel?

_____
_____
_____
_____
_____

5. What would it take to know you are worthy of everything you say you want?

_____
_____
_____
_____
_____
_____

6. How seriously do you value your physical health, your emotions and thoughts? What do you value the most about yourself?

_____
_____
_____
_____
_____
_____

7. Do you constantly need to be reminded that you are worthy of love, kindness and respect? Are you insecure about yourself?

_____
_____
_____
_____

8. Do you lack confidence? So you suffer from self loathing?

_____
_____
_____
_____
_____

9. Do you create conflicts? Are you cynical and doubting?

_____
_____
_____
_____
_____
_____-

10. Do you believe you are worthy simply because you exist? Do you feel you have to prove your worth?

_____
_____
_____
_____
_____
_____

11. Can you connect with the place within yourself where you know you are good?

Can you allow your light to shine and be a beacon that others can see from afar?

_____
_____
_____
_____
_____
_____
_____

12. Do you feel that if you were different in some way (older/younger/fatter/thinner/ blonde/whiter/kinder/more spiritual, etc) you would be more entitled to kindness and consideration?

Again, ask yourself what it takes for you to consider yourself worthy ?

Can you accept yourself as you are or do you need to change something about yourself?

_____
_____
_____
_____
_____
_____
_____

13. Do you feel you have to change in order to be worthy? Do you have to please others to be worthy? Your parents? Mother? Partner or spouse? Your children? Colleagues? Business associates?

_____
_____
_____
_____
_____
_____

14. Can you see this is a delusion? Does it really matter what others think of you?

_____
_____
_____
_____-

15. What does it take to value yourself? Are you worthy of what you say you want? What is lacking in your life that defines your worth?

_____
_____
_____
_____
_____
_____
_____-

16. Can you call to mind people or situations where you have honored your self and allowed your light to shine? What has been the results?

_____
_____
_____
_____
_____
_____
_____
_____
_____

17. Do you feel conflicted and challenged relating to successful people? Do you trust people to be on your side? Do you believe someone can watch your back in times of distress?

_____
_____
_____
_____
_____
_____
_____
_____
_____
_____

18. Do you collude with others in undermining your self ? Do you put yourself down ? Do you denigrate yourself? How do you feel when you are negative about yourself?

_____
_____
_____
_____
_____
_____
_____
_____

19. Do you believe the negative things others say about you? Do you stop their insults? Do you walk away? Do you tell them how hurtful their remarks are to you? Do you buy into their negativity?

_____
_____
_____
_____
_____
_____
_____

20. Do you harbor hatred and resentment for negative things others say about you? Do you stand up for yourself? Do you treat others with kindness, consideration, care and attention? Can your shrug off others' hurtful remarks and just allow them to be who they are?

_____
_____
_____
_____
_____
_____
_____
_____

Self Esteem:

What distinguishes self worth from self esteem is the latter is associated with the things we do and the achievements we have made. It means we are proud of ourselves. Self worth is how we value ourselves and honor our intrinsic worth as a human being.

1. Can you list the things which you are proud of having done in your life?

_____
_____
_____
_____
_____
_____

2. What has given you the greatest sense of pride?
_____
_____
_____
_____

3. Why are you proud of that? What does this represent to you?
_____
_____
_____
_____
_____
_____

4. What would you like others to know that makes you proud of yourself? Are you trustworthy? Can you be counted on? Are you a good friend to others? Do you help others? Can you get the job done?
_____
_____
_____
_____
_____

5. Do you reward yourself for the things you are proud of? Do you dismiss your efforts? Do you punish yourself and say you could have done better?
_____
_____
_____
_____

6. What gives you a sense of pride in yourself?
_____
_____
_____
_____-

Confidence:

Confidence: when you develop confidence it permeates every area of your life. It reflects in simple ways and shows up in how you take risks and meet challenges.

1. Are you confident that you are good enough for the things you want?
_____
_____
_____
_____
_____

2. Do you feel that more education, more money, better cloths , better car, or a bigger house will give you more confidence in yourself ? What gives you confidence in yourself and tells you that you are worthy?
_____
_____
_____

3. What takes away your confidence? What enhances it?

_____
_____
_____
_____
_____
_____

4. What gives you confidence? A friendly face? A kind word? A phone call from someone who cares? How you look? How you feel getting the job done?

_____
_____
_____
_____
_____
_____
_____

5. What makes you feel good? Do you have what it takes to meet the tasks at hand? Are you confident? Assured? Positive and optimistic?

_____
_____
_____
_____
_____
_____

6. Do you feel confident in relationships? Work situations? Family? Friends? Partners? Where is your confidence high ? Where is it low?
_____
_____
_____
_____
_____
_____

Part One: Chapter Three

WORKBOOK PAGES:

The idea for this workbook is to give you an opportunity to explore your thoughts, feelings, memories and work situations. Releasing anger, fear, doubt, cynicism opens channels for growth and healing. Use this workbook to help you get to know yourself.

Write down your impressions, open your heart to express your pain and sorrow and free yourself of the burden of carrying guilt, shame and the emotions they engender.

This is for you.

1. How do you feel about releasing the hold shame , guilt and martyrdom have over you? Do you feel positive or uncertain? Do you feel negative and hopeless?

_____
_____
_____
_____
_____
_____
_____
_____

2. What do you want to release now? How has this limited you?

_____
_____
_____
_____
_____
_____
_____
_____
_____
_____
_____
_____

3. Can you release your anger? Can you forgive those you blame? Write it down and release your feelings.

_____
_____
_____
_____
_____

4. What do you need to say to the people who caused you to feel shame and guilt? This is an opportunity for you to experience clarity.

_____
_____

Meditation:

Meditation is the practice of being still; physically, emotionally and mentally. It affords you the experience of being at peace. We meditate to quiet the mind, relax our over stressed nervous system, and find tranquility .

Meditation helps you detach from worldly involvement. It puts you within the boundaries of your own inner being, feeling good in your skin, and able to transcend the boundaries of your mind that limit your thinking or suppress your emotions.

Meditation is designed to bring tranquility, clarity, focus and stability. It begins by sitting quietly and comfortably ,paying attention to your breath. Rest your back on a comfortable cushions or against a wall. Be at ease as you breathe in through your nose . Fill your lungs with air before you release your breath; in and out , in and out . In through your nose, out through your nose. Do this slowly and rhythmically until you feel relaxed, at ease and in the moment.

Draw the air in deeply and feel your body begin to let go of tension and ease down. Let your jaw drop , and your mouth feel relaxed. Relax your tongue as it falls into the back of your throat.

Feel the tension behind your eyes soften and your temples relax. Feel the back of your neck and your shoulders loosen .

Imagine tension leaving your body out through your feet and hands. You begin to feel lighter and more at ease. Stay focused on your breathing. Keep letting go .

When you are calm and stillness settles into your being feel your spirit expand . It spreads out through your physical body and then begin to experience the internal shifts as fear, anger, shame and guilt melt and dissolve. You feel well in yourself as your spirit releases those tense places where you hold your negativity .

Feel your spirit soothe and comfort you with love, warmth, kindness , grace and mercy . It eases your tension and dissolves your pain.

Let go of tension, anxiety, and release your fears. If you need to weep give yourself permission. Often a good cry frees the tension you hold onto. It helps you let go of frustration.

Practice sitting in meditation daily , even for a few minutes. Do it when you get up or before sleep. Do it when you wake up and /or at night before sleep. Let your spirit love you, heal you and release you from what blocks your happiness.

Love the spirit that lives in you and longs for you to be well. It flows out of your heart in all directions, filling your being with grace. It loves you because it is a part of you.

Your spirit offers you strength, love, wisdom for the asking. Expand your capacity to know how your spirit serves your needs and helps you enjoy moments of ease and rest. It only requires you to be still and allow healing to happen. Open up and listen.

When you are ready to connect with the world around you bring your attention back into the present moment. Open your eyes, be still, be grateful. Enjoy your day.

Affirmations:

Affirmations are a way of stating positive intentions. You can repeat them often, write them several times a day, sing them, do them swimming or jogging. Say the ones that ring true for you. They will help you re-program your mind to be fully affirmative and positive. It takes three weeks of daily repetition to anchor an affirmation into the sub conscious mind where it becomes habit.

You can say them using an ancient arm crossing method that stimulates the acupuncture meridians and anchors your affirmations into your body.

It is a powerful technique for affirmations.

You do this by crossing your arms over your chest. Now say an affirmation out loud. Take the bottom arm out and cross it over the top arm.

Again , say an affirmation with your arms crossed over your chest. When you have completed it take the bottom arm and place it over the top arm. Repeat this each time you say an affirmation.

When you are done flap both hands on your shoulders as if you are saying " well done!" Pat yourself on the shoulders.

This technique was taught to me by Teri Kosmicki, a gifted healer.

Here are affirmations that release shame, guilt and martyrdom.

I RELEASE SHAME AND GUILT FROM MY BEING. THEY NO LONGER SERVE ME.

I AM NOT A VICTIM OR A MARTYR.

I LOVE AND RESPECT MYSELF .

I KNOW MY VALUE AS A PERSON.

I STOP ALL SELF PUNISHMENT.

I RELEASE A BELIEF IN PUNISHMENT .

I FORGIVE MYSELF FOR DENYING MY TRUE NATURE.

I NOW TREAT MYSELF WITH LOVE AND RESPECT IN ALL SITUATIONS.

I LOVE THE HEART AND SOUL OF MY BEING.

I WILLING RELEASE MY NEGATIVE BELIEFS. THEY DISSOVLE INTO THE NOTHINGNESS FROM WHERE THEY CAME.

I KNOW I AM WORTHY OF LOVE , KINDNESS AND RESPECT. I START BY LOVING MYSELF.

I GIVE MYSELF PERMISSION TO ENJOY LIFE.

I AM ONE WITH MY CREATOR. I KNOW I AM LOVED , HONORED AND CHERISHED .

NO ONE HAS THE RIGHT TO DIMINISH OR ABUSE ME.

I STAND UP FOR MYSELF OUT OF SELF RESPECT AND I LOVE WHO I AM.

I AM WORTHY OF THE LIFE I SAY I WANT.

I CLAIM MY GOOD NOW.

I ALLOW PLEASURE AND GOODNESS TO FLOW IN MY LIFE.

I TRUST IN THE WHOLEHEARTED GOODNESS OF LIFE .

I INVITE LOVE TO FIND ME.

Create your own affirmations. Stand firm in your belief for your right to the life you say you want. Think absolute and perfect health, unlimited prosperity, deep , abiding love and beautiful self expression. Its all there for you to claim right now.

Visualization:

Visualization works by creating visual images of the life you want to manifest. It employs both sides of the brain, using your creative and imaginative right hemisphere of the brain for your desires and the rational , calculating and measuring left brain for the form you wish to see manifest.

Visualization is a powerful tool to create what you long for and desire. You see the image in your mind's eye of what you want and imbue that image with emotion and feeling. See yourself enjoying life: healthy, wealthy , loved and enjoying full self expression. Claim the images that appeal to you.

Begin a visualization by being in a comfortable place where you feel safe and at ease. Feel the comfort of your surroundings, delight in being where you are. Imagine a tray of your favorite treats in front of you. There are all the goodies you enjoy. Pick one you particularly like and imagine yourself eating it. Imagine the texture of it, the flavor, the crunchy or smooth texture. Conjure up the details about this that delights you. Can you imagine how delicious this is?

Another exercise is to imagine you just heard you have won a big prize. It is a lot of money and a ticket to anywhere you wish to go. What do you want to do with this money? Where do you want to go? Think about it. Get some photos off the web and see yourself there. Ask yourself who would you go with ? By yourself or with a friend? Can you see yourself in First Class on a plane, ship , train, or hired car ? You feel excited about this adventure. You re dressed for it in your mind's eye. You are ready to thoroughly enjoy yourself.

Imagine the hotel you ll stay at or the house you'll rent. See the gardens, the furniture , feel the ambiance. Isn't it lovely? Comfortable? Better than you can imagine?

Visualize yourself walking around the town or village near your lodgings. Stop for a moment and look at the shop windows.

What captures your fancy? What would you like to purchase with the money you just won?

See yourself enjoying a delicious meal that is beyond anything you ever experienced in a good restaurant. Visualize excellent cuisine, happy conversations with friends or simply being alone , quiet and taking it all in. All this is a gift for being you.

Perhaps you want to purchase something big with your winnings. It may be a car, a boat, , a jet plane. You can have anything you wish. What will it be? What color? What size? Is it vintage? Is it brand new?

You may wish to be in nature, in a forest, at the beach, on a mountain. Claim the experience by seeing yourself there. You are free, happy, and delighted being in the glory of this beautiful scenery.

Keep imagining what you would do with this enormous prize: quit your day job? Invest in a wonderful , innovative project? Buy a new home? Share this money with people who could use a leg up? The choice is yours. All you are asked to do is imagine the wonderful experience of having whatever it is you wish.

Repeat this exercise until you can focus on what it is you want to manifest. Then clarify your intention and hold the visualization in your mind's eye, Repeat this visualization for three weeks until it is locked into your mind and you can pull up the image at any time. You can write the script so you recall the same image every day. Make any amendments necessary to give your visualization a unique look.

Visualizations have a peculiar way of coming true . The more you practice and refine your images the more likely it is you will manifest exactly what it is you see in your mind's eye.

You can also do visualization for experiencing inner qualities you may be lacking . Start with feeling pride and confidence in who you are. Know you are loved and worthy of whatever you say you want. Feel confident in your visualization, rested, relaxed, enjoying the feeling you wish to create.

Love yourself and embrace your vision. Release your doubt, anger, and mistrust . Don't let it lurk in the recesses of your mind. Remind yourself you are finished with negative thoughts and allow them to disappear.

Focus on being loved, winning in life, having radiant health, fabulous wealth, faithful love and perfect self expression. Imagine everything you could ever dream of having in your life right now.

Every day can be a prize in the lottery of life. Take time to reflect what it is you want to manifest. Learn to love yourself and feel wonderful every day so you release the blocks to what you want manifesting. Bless the day when you awake and know it is complete. Affirm miracle follows miracle and wonders never cease. Release anything that holds you down or demands you do something that displeases you. For a moment forget about rules that limit and constrict you. Live life on your terms in your mind's eye. Feel what that is like? Even see yourself flying in the clouds or over beautiful terrain.

You were chosen by your Creator to enjoy something good every day. Let it be as simple as feeling the joy of life, the wonder of creation and the uniqueness of your being. Look around you and feel how deeply blessed you are. Give thanks for the good you do have right now.

Have fun creating your world just the way you want it to be. Don't be too surprised when it comes true over time. The power of your imagination and the wonder of your intentions ignites a spark in the universe to deliver your desires and bring you what you want .

Prayer:

Prayer is an appeal to the Creator for help. Use prayer as part of your healing. Ask the Lord and His angels to bless you, guide you, offer healing and help you to release your personal baggage of shame, guilt and martyrdom.

There is nothing that can not be done through the power of prayer and nothing that can not be forgiven. It is so powerful when people congregate to offer prayers, or when " two or more people gather in my Name," as Christ said to ask for what they want and need.

Our intentions, whether gathered in affirmations, visualizations, or focused in meditation or revealed through prayer, have power. The greatest of these powers is the ability to connect with Source and become co-creator with your life. Prayer goes deep to that level of spiritual connection.

There is nothing that has to be done to make an appeal. Ask for what you want and remember you are always connected. You are worthy of what you say you want. Have faith the good is unfolding for you now.

You can light candles, incense, make a clean and beautiful space. That is all trim. What really matters is your willingness to be humble and grateful for the good you have experienced and ask for help. You are never refused.

Here are prayers to release shame , guilt and martyrdom and free you to enjoy life.

BELOVED , Please hear my prayer that I may be released from the taint of shame, the disenfranchisement of guilt and the drudgery of martyrdom. I wish to live a good life, free, open, adventurous, courageous. I ask for laughter, warmth and love. Help me put away negative thinking that leaves me unhappy , sad and lost.

Thank you for your love, for your kindness and generosity. I am grateful. Amen

Beloved , open me to receive the blessing of freedom . Help me live my life on my terms, unafraid to walk through life upright, contributing where and how I can . I wish to make my patch of the universe a better place.

Thank you for your guidance, your trust in my ability to do good . Help me make wholesome choices for myself and those I love. Amen.

Beloved, I offer you thanks for walking along side of me through this patch of thorns. I pray that you heal my wounds, melt my anger , dissolve my rage and enmity . Give me another chance to be and do the best I can, in love, trust and the desire to do good. I am yours. Thank you for all the goodness that flows to me. Amen.

Beloved Self, I give thanks for the knowledge you hold and that you embrace me in your arms , guide me to the light , offer me the good I seek. I release my doubts, fears and self consciousness. I let go and know I am fine without any embellishment . I thank you for your strength and your guidance , your love and mercy. Thank you.

Part Two

Pleasure - The Cornerstone of Health

Part Two: Chapter Four

Cultivating Pleasure and Ease

Ancient Egyptians honored their river god who was known as Sobek. They fed him ample amounts of fish in the hopes of pacifying him . He represented the forces of pleasure, ease and leisure.

They felt if the god was not treated to his favorite dishes he would turn his wrath on the population;fear, death, and chaos would ensue.

Buddhists also believe in a mythical type of sea monster that resides deep within the human belly. This monster resembles Sobek in that he, too, requires constant feeding. In some Buddhist rituals they offer up food to the god to keep him happy.

They know that a lifestyle that is too rigid and punishing creates desire along with a sense of deprivation. They believe by filling one's life with enough pleasure to stave off sadness, depression and grief and encourage a person to enjoy a happy, balanced life .

The Buddha called this " the Middle Way." They believe in feeding the senses but not being attached to them in the process. They encourage moderation in all things .

In truth, it is pleasure that keeps us stable and our lives flowing in the direction of the good. It is important to include pleasure , ease and rest in our daily life , especially during times of challenge. This means allowing time to let down, rest, eat good nurturing food, and have free time away from worry and stress.

We need to take breaks from hard work and demanding tasks. We ease down , find comfort in simple pleasures and forget our troubles for a brief while before we pick them back up and carry them again.

It is pleasure that opens the heart; and goodness that eases the mind. Momentarily we are given relief from the grind. We find time to recover our strength and move forward with ease.

Deprivation is hard on the spirit; it weighs us down, it constipates the spirit and dries out the soul. It reminds us we are in lack and creates a longing for things we don't have.

By allowing ourselves pleasure we participate in the ebb and flow of life. We keep life simple, uncomplicated and enjoyable . Pleasure eases the spirit and soothes stressed nerves. It is a wise person who knows what they need to keep themselves on an even keel. Pleasure builds inner awareness, deepens our trust of Self and adds to our maturity.

As we develop our connection to spirit and build higher levels of self esteem we expand our capacity for more pleasure. We release old , stale beliefs about pleasure when we ease down and enjoy a pleasurable moment .

A lack of pleasure weakens us and destroys our sense of the sweetness of life. Drudgery hardens us, and makes our burdens feel heavier . When you walk in grace, you allow the good to flow. This happens regardless of your age ,or your circumstances.

This is the beginning of mastering the art of living. It takes time and experience to perfect so keep practicing and be patient. Learn to allow yourself the pleasures you enjoy.

Embracing the good counteracts all negativity. Whatever beliefs you absorbed from your family, school or religious institutions or the strict punishing you received, dictates how your culture of inner growth is learning that you are entitled to enjoy your life.

Many of the principles we live by are punishing, restrictive and counter the the goodness of natural ease. Learn to believe you are worthy of happiness and joy. Invite pleasure and ease into your daily life. Allow the divine to bless you.

The old ideas put fear into people, telling them they are unworthy and not good enough for what they want. We each have to untie the knots of punishment we have absorbed. Its up to each of us to find a way to a life that fulfills our gifts, honors our talents and gives us permission to be happy.

As you allow yourself to enjoy the good you will want more of it . If you can allow it you will ask for more of what you want. Make room for happiness every day; cultivate it, teach yourself you are worthy and expand your capacity to be happy .

This stops destructive ideas about self sacrifice and unworthiness. As you start embracing your life you will find gratitude for the amazing experiences and wonderful people you encounter. You will learn that everything is a blessing.

You will have your attitudes about happiness and joy challenged ,as well as your beliefs questioned. If you expect confirmation from the world you are likely to be disappointed. It is up to you to honor your claim to happiness, claim wealth , demand good health and the deep joy of creative expression. No one can do this for you or give you permission. You must find it in yourself.

As you let go of self limiting beliefs ask yourself if you are worthy of what you want. Allow your self worth to define you, rather than your negativity, fear, and oppressive life style . Expand your capacity for joy.

You are happier when you love yourself and think the best of who you are . Let go of cruel, punishing thoughts. Forgive yourself, make peace with your past, and walk in grace . Let divine love soften the hard places of fear; let the Holy Spirit open you to the beauty and goodness that abides everywhere, especially within yourself.

Be aware that self love is not conditional on what you do or what you have. It comes from knowing you are worthy simply because you exist. You are a being of light, a child of the Creator and your abilty to enjoy your relationship to joy and happiness carries your light into the world.

You are free to choose your path as a light bearer. You are soul and spirit worthy of experiencing your innate goodness. Your joy is there to be claimed, blessed and honored.

It is up to you to value your true self. Only you can know how sacred your life is. You are invited to call the good to you .When you know you are worthy and the universe wants you to succeed you can literally manifest whatever you want.

The more you treat yourself with respect and love the stronger and more resilient your foundation for goodness becomes.

Begin by paying attention to your needs ; you can choose the good by giving yourselves rest, peace, love and affection . You can put healthy boundaries in place and say no to what drags you down. Learn to protect your energy and insure the sanctity of your life.

Western culture has defined you by the type and amount of work you do, but it is pleasure that molds your spirit. Pleasure keeps your physical engines oiled and your spirit strong.

Observe people who carry heavy burdens and you ll see how they struggle with concepts like " relaxation", " ease", "pleasure and joy". Their burdens limit their capacity for good to flow to them. The Christ said " come to me for my yoke is easy and my burdens light."

The Christ is the living presence within you. In Hebrew the Christ consciousness is called "Yud Hey Vav Hey" or I AM THAT I AM. This is the force of the indelible soul. It comes from the blessing of the Most High. When you want healing this is where you turn.

Surrender your problems, trust the good and allow what you want and need to come to you. Let yourself ease down into joy, goodness and pleasure.

The mark of adulthood is being vigilant, responsible and dutiful.

A person who can do what it takes to get the job done well is also given permission to choose what delights him, what feels good and what will fulfill and nourish his spirit.

It is time you choose the people and things you love. Expand your spirit . Without pleasure the spirit shrivels and your become old and enfeebled very quickly . Your mind becomes dull, your body wears down and disease finds its way in.

Be responsible for your welfare ,do what makes you happy and gives you pleasure .Keep it simple, effortless and relaxing. Well adjusted people add pleasure into the equation of their daily lives. They know how to make it work for them to live with minimal stress, difficulties or accidents . That is taking responsibility for pleasure.

Healthy people know when they need a break from the routine of work and stress . They give themselves time off; and do things they enjoy. Their intention is to revive their spirit in ease and pleasure.

Learn to grow in delight. See yourself accepting ease and pleasure. It is the reward for living .

When people invalidate this need for self care and pleasure they lose a healthy perspective on life. Work teaches you focus; it teaches you to take control of situations and manage people and circumstances.

Pleasure teaches you to let go , be in the moment, and enjoy the flow of life. It stimulates the " feel good" endorphins that act as a tonic to your nervous system. Pleasure is the other half of hard work.

Once you integrate these polar opposite forces into your life you create balance for yourself. Loving your work and taking time for pleasure is a recipe for health and happiness. Pleasure prepares you for more work; and work offers the rewards of ease and fun.

Learn to enjoy yourself . Consider new ways to find joy in life . It is as much an attitude as an activity.

People who are constantly striving, afraid to let go or ease up on control are run by fear. They are consumed by guilt at not being enough. At some deep level there is shame , the horror of not being in control or not being perfect. If the don't halt the neurotic litany running their mind they will grind themselves down and burn out. There is no amount of caffeine, dope, alcohol, sex, or any other addictive substance that replaces self care.

THE INDIVIDUALITY OF PLEASURABLE PURSUITS

Pleasure is an individual experience . It is dependent on what you find pleasing, delightful and what makes your heart sing . Pleasure is molded by a person's nature and what attracts them. It s always about what you enjoy and love doing.

Its your job to find out what does and does not bring you pleasure. It also takes time to explore the realm of possibilities regarding what is pleasing to you .

For some people pleasure is as simple as watching a child play, or sitting quietly in a beautiful garden reading a book. It may be simply feeling good about what the day brings and going with the flow . For others it involves active sport, hard workouts and daring adventure.

It's always good to know what you like and enjoy. Make a list of twenty things that you enjoy. It can be as simple as reading the paper over a cup of coffee, listening to a radio program, planting a garden, laughing with friends. Different pleasures depending on time of day, weather conditions, geographical localities, the people you enjoy doing things with and a multitude of other factors that help you differentiate what delights you.

It may take time to develop a repertoire of things you enjoy but it is always worth knowing what puts a twinkle in your eyes and a smile on your face. Know what has the power to delight you. Pleasure is always enjoyment without guilt or shame.

Pleasure has the ability to blow away the cobwebs from your tired mind and releases the pressure of high performance activity. Pleasure expands the neuro-pathways of the brain. It stimulates your breath , charges your blood and releases the feel good hormones know as endorphins. It rejuvenates you and brings you home to center.

Pleasure gives you a sense of lightness and ignites your age defying spirit. You thrive on pleasure because it satisfies your senses, delights your spirit and strengthens your heart. Pleasure is the sweetness we never tire of.

Say yes to what makes you happy. Know what is enough and when its time to stop playing and get back to work. You don't want to glut your senses, tire yourself out or overstimulate your nervous system.

Being sated from too much pleasure makes you constipated and lazy. It's a wise person who knows the right measure of when enough is enough. Learn to know what your limit is regarding time out from stress.

At its best pleasure is a resource you cultivate to build a strong platform of things to enjoy when you need to relax. Sometimes doing nothing is the best medicine for a tired spirit. Other times you can choose an activity that pleases you.

Pleasure is the stop gap between the battles of life. It regenerates your strength so you can master the next task. Without pleasure you stagnate and lose control of the very situations you wish to master. Find the balance between doing and being. Learn to relax and find your ease.

Allowing Goodness

The key to pleasure is allowing it to happen, giving it space to unfold, without controlling it. Stop denying what you need or pretending you don't need to relax. Only an egotist would tell you they don't need rest, ease or to take a break doing something pleasurable.

If you can allow yourself pleasure without guilt or shame you have achieved a high level of personal development and self worth. When you cultivate a healthy attitude towards pleasure you strengthen your immunity ten fold. Pleasure and ease keep you on track. They heal and restore you and remind you that you are worthy of the good.

There is intelligence in knowing when to rest, slowing down the pace and easing down into pleasure . It conserves your energy to rest before you extend your physical and mental resources.

Learn to take the pressure off, relax your " fight or flight" reflexes that controls adrenaline flow. Pleasure and ease preserve your kidneys, calm anxiety , expand the lungs and enrich your blood with oxygen. The heart loves pleasure. Pleasure ultimately fortifies your physical , mental and emotional health.

Constant assault on the nerves leads to burn out. Without respite and ease the system becomes chronically weak. With too much striving you lose stamina, diminish resiliency and compromise vitality.

You may think you have a super human will that allows you to drive yourself unceasingly without respite. This is a delusion. The body quickly demonstrates its finite capacity for action and intolerance for stress when pushed too hard. It actually becomes numb and dysfunctional. Look at the autoimmune illnesses actors and high profile business people contract. It all starts with burn out and a failure to listen to the body's need for peace and rest.

Health is conditional on strong kidneys, a well functioning liver and a vibrant, healthy heart,.

Most of all, it needs a strong nervous system where nerve fibers are coated with a fatty substance called Myelin .

As Myelin wears down with age, medications, recreational drugs and workaholic behavior you lose the ability to think clearly and function physically. Myelin is the key to physical stamina, strength and good health. It is said when the nervous system goes there is no returning to good health. That is the point of being up against the wall without recourse to recovery. Its the time when changes must be made for self preservation.

We want to build a strong nervous system that feeds and nourishes the physical body and balances out our mental and emotional health.

If you are in this state please stop coffee, drugs and stimulants, and taking meds that alter your state of mind. Consult a doctor before you take this on . It requires professional guidance to stop being an adrenaline addict.

Myelin is built by regular motion such as playing a musical instrument, repetitive sports practices and daily meditation.

Pleasure is physical

Pleasure is not ethereal, nor is it spiritual; it is essentially physical. It requires a physical body capable of feeling that has strong , healthy nerve receptors, and a good receptive mind capable of processing experiences without shame or guilt. Pleasure asks for a spirit that appreciates experiences. It needs a being that is strong enough to reverse negative thinking so good prevails.

Pleasure melts fat, which acts as a shield to high levels of acidity . Acid destroys the mucus membranes in the digestive track, creating ulcers and lesions.

Pleasure endorphins help metabolize food and aid in the digestive process. Constipation is a sign of fatigue and over work. Diarrhea is a sign of anxiety and worry.

Pleasure endorphins reduce cholesterol and help restore and replenish vitality. You can build a strong immune system when you engage in pleasurable pursuits. An energetic principle says "you expand in pleasure and contract in pain."

Make pleasure compatible with your right to goodness. It softens the hard edges and makes you receptive to positive change . It reminds you how good life is . It can get you through the hard times.

Joy is a natural state of being and it delights the heart. The heart longs for pleasure; it wants to laugh, love and feel good. Pleasure is the key to joy. Heart health is giving yourself the loving energy the heart longs for and needs. Your blood flows better when you are happy and doing what you enjoy.

Allowing pleasure expands your spirit and increases your capacity for wholehearted goodness . By accepting pleasure you affirm you are worthy. You start to release drudgery and end the battle for survival. This is a great accomplishment.

When you affirm your right to pleasure say "Thank you, I know I am worth it! " When you eliminate shame and guilt celebrate how good that feels . Enjoy feeling the ease of loving kindness, tender mercy, and true sweetness. The rhythm is slow , satisfying and fulfilling.

Pleasure, Energy and Reserves

To build a healthy foundation where pleasure can thrive you want to construct a consistant practice where you call pleasure and ease into your life. Ask for joy to find you and listen for it coming in many different forms. Its in the the sweet sound of birdsong early in the morning. Its the sound of children playing. Look for it in moments of grace and beauty and where you least expect it. Laugh when there is something funny. Learn to delight in the good instead of ignoring it or complaining about minor irritations. Joy, pleasure and ease want to be experienced as often as possible.

The more self love you have the easier it is to accept pleasure and chose ease . It becomes easier to let go and relax. Pleasure seldom computes for people who are filled with self loathing and punishment. They drive themselves into exhaustion.

Self love lets you rest in silence, find peace, have time to reflect and make positive choices for your good. Ease and pleasure are essential components to happiness.

Pleasure, ease and joy are like Blue Chip stocks. You put that energy away in reserve for challenging times when you need it . You remember the good and you know you want more of it. You ll want moments of enjoyment , ease and pleasure regularly They sustain your spirit and expand your sense of goodness.

Pleasure can be as regular as a weekly golf game or meeting friends in the pub . It can be as regular as a daily workout, or making time for a good movie or your favorite radio program. Pleasure is basically simple and it can keep you healthy for years.

Pleasure also makes you aware of who, and what drain your vitality. Too many tense people too much of the time suck the air out of the room; they deplete your reserves and they wear you down.

Learn to construct healthy boundaries to protect yourself from negative, needy, or angry people. Don't become attached to their state of mind. If you have chronic stress from work or relationships it may be time to make a life style change that is compatible with your new sense of self worth.

The mental signs of chronic stress are confusion, memory loss, irritation and, even, obsession. There may be physical symptoms such as high blood pressure, heart failure, chronic headaches, chronic constipation or diarrhea.

When you are tired, irritated and fed up what transforms your energy is ease and pleasure . This is what regenerates you. When you are low or life weighs heavily, pleasure revives . It is through pleasure you are renewed ,ready to fight the good fight once again.

How We Rejuvenate

Rejuvenating the body and healing the spirit require internal shifts of perception . It also takes patience.

First, get a handle on harvesting out your negativity; take responsibility for your choices, forgive yourself for getting hooked into bad decisions that depleted and diminished you. Pay attention to judgment, criticism, and underlying anger that block your well being.

Start to build a life that is positive. Affirm you are capable of joy; someone able to appreciate beauty and enjoy pleasure. This sustains you through hard times and helps heal pain, separation, trauma and loss.

You have a right to pleasure. Pleasure, love, success and abundance are part of the package we develop through self love.

Knowing your innate worth puts an end to self abuse and servitude; it stops you being depleted and diminished. No one can force you into martyrdom. Its your choice to see the world through this archetypal optic. And it is your choice to transform this archetype to a higher, more conscious one that supports your happiness and well being.

When you make good choices for yourself you expand your capacity for joy and allow goodness to find you. Consider what you do and with whom you do it. Are these people life enhancing or do they deplete you. Do they take you down or lead you to higher ground? You can make pleasure a sustainable experience with long term roots that anchor you in the good. You can pray for kind people who love you as you are without using, abusing or manipulating you to come into your life.

Pleasure Retards the Aging Process

The happier you are the more beautiful you are. Happy people radiate light. Nothing ages a person more than misery, unhappiness and stress . Beauty is the reflection of your inner light , it reflects your capacity to give and recieve love, find joy and gratitude for life . Beauty reflects a person making wholesome choices for themselves .

What keeps you vibrant and healthy for years is abiding love in your self, and trusting the divine to see you through. Being open to love, joy and pleasure fills your heart and occupy your mind with positive energy.

The older you get the more you want to choose pleasure and allow the good into your life . It is soul enhancing as well as life preserving .

As you increase your capacity to deal with life's challenges you come to appreciate the importance of fun, pleasure and joy . They are fundamental for internal stability; they keep you moving forward in the direction of life.

They allow you to experience the best of yourself and help you make room in your life for lasting happiness.

Claim Your Good

In order to claim your good you must believe that what you long for and desire is possible to attain. Hold it in your mind that what you desire is within the realm of possibility for you to have. Say "YES" to your dreams . Affirm your sense of worthiness to have what you want.

Claim the inner qualities you need to enjoy your dreams. Open up to the possibility of emotional stability, real happiness, good health, abundant wealth, true love and wonderful creative expression .

Give the good permission to flow easily and effortlessly in and through your life .Let it come quickly, easily, under grace and in perfect ways. What you claim is not an external thing. In truth, it is a state of being you want to manifest.

You are responsible for your happiness and finding pleasure in life. This includes creating meaningful work that gets you out of bed in the morning, a healthy , joyful and loving relationship that can handle the ups and downs in life, stable finances, and optimal health. In other words: its up to you to choose the good and trust in life to see you through. Faith is knowing that what you want will manifest.

It all begins with believing you are worthy of your heart's desire and it is possible to have that which you seek. Pleasure can only be experienced by those who believe it is theirs to enjoy. No one can convince a person about their worthiness, or how important ease and pleasure are for health .It comes from inner knowing.

Whatever it takes to develop this consciousness is a worthy investment in your psychological growth and spiritual development. Do the inner work of establishing a healthy emotional foundation, learn patience, trust, and faith that it will come to be.

This form of transformation opens the path to a good life because it builds character. It helps you mature and trust in life.

All it requires is a change of perception , a willingness to release blame, guilt and shame and a desire to see the good around you. A healthy dose of forgiveness also goes a long way in opening the channels of good to flow.

Could you have made your life less painful and more pleasurable? Probably. Could you have chosen love rather than enmity? Most likely. Could you reframe those negative moments, ask for forgiveness and heal your heart? Hopefully.

Life is an amazing journey that gives you endless opportunities to turn muck into gold. That gold is deeply connected to allowing pleasure and the good to be incorporated into your life.

It takes knowing you are worthy of real love, deep, lasting happiness and the best for yourself to turn your sour experiences into sweet ones. Let go of the addiction to drama and misery. Let go of a belief in self punishment and release a desire for revenge for those who hurt or abused you. Chose to define yourself in a happier , more pleasurable way.

Part Two: Chapter Five

A Practicum: Questions, Meditation, Affirmations, Visualization and Prayer

Questions:

Take time to reflect on your responses to these questions. If you wish to make changes in your life ask yourself what you want . Then do the inner work of meditation, affirmation, visualization and prayer to improve your life.

1. Do you feel you have a right to enjoy yourself?

2. What would you enjoy doing daily? Weekly? Monthly ? Every few months to bring more pleasure into your life?

_____
_____
_____
_____
_____
_____
_____
_____
_____

3. Do you have a strong, well developed sense of your right to pleasure?

_____
_____

4. How can you expand your repertoire of pleasurable experiences?

_____
_____
_____
_____

5. List the things you would enjoy doing?

_____
_____
_____
_____
_____
_____
_____

6. What else would you enjoy?

_____

7. Are there skills you would like to cultivate?

_____

8. Are there people you want to meet?

_____

9. Are there places you would like to visit?

_____

10. Are there foods you d like to taste? Shows you want to see? Music you would enjoy hearing?

_____
_____
_____
_____
_____
_____
_____
_____

11. Can you give yourself permission to expand your capacity for joy and pleasure?

_____

12. What more would you like to do?

_____
_____
_____
_____
_____
_____
_____
_____
_____

13. What delights you?

_____
_____
_____
_____
_____

14. How well do you take care of yourself?

_____

15. Do you get enough rest? Do you eat good quality food? Do you enjoy your down time? Do you take time off to enjoy yourself? Do you have a rich personal life? Do you enjoy your friends and companions?

_____
_____
_____
_____
_____
_____
_____
_____
_____

16. How would you expand your schedule to include more joy and ease?

_____
_____
_____
_____

17. How do you limit your self in regards to pleasure and ease?

_____

18. How do you avoid imagining the life you say you want?

_____
_____
_____
_____
_____
_____

19. What are your fears around having ease and pleasure in your life?

_____

20, Do you see it as indulgence?

_____

21. Do you think people will criticize you for having pleasure and ease in your life?

_____
_____
_____
_____
_____
_____
_____

22. Do you fear you will overdo the good times and regret it?

_____
_____
_____

23.. Are your pleasures physical, emotional, mental or spiritual in nature?

_____
_____
_____
_____
_____

24. What type of pleasurable experiences are you most comfortable with?

_____
_____
_____
_____
_____

25. If an opportunity for pleasure presented itself to you right now would you allow yourself to enjoy it? What would be your reasons for saying no to it?

_____
_____
_____
_____
_____
_____
_____

26. Are you able to turn a tedious chore into a pleasurable experience?

_____

27. What would make your day more enjoyable?
_____
_____
_____
_____
_____

28.. If pleasure was conditional on you giving up something you valued, would you do that ? What would you be willing to give up?
_____
_____
_____
_____
____-

29. Are you seduced by the promise of pleasure?
_____
_____
_____

30. Do you allow yourself the pleasures you want ?
_____
_____
_____

31. Do you share your pleasure with others or are you singular in your pursuit of ease and joy?

_____
_____
_____
_____
___

32. Do you take life seriously or do you find life humorous?

_____
_____
_____
_____
_____
_____
___ _____

33. Are you clear what your boundaries are regarding pleasure?

_____
_____
_____
_____
_____
_____
_____
_____

34. How would you fill your days with pleasure?

_____
_____
_____
_____
_____
_____
_____-

35. How much pleasure is dependent upon what others share with you? How much is self generated?

_____
_____
_____
_____
_____
_____
_____

36. What are your good memories of pleasurable times?

_____
_____
_____
_____
_____
_____
_____
_____
_____

37. What would you change in the future to allow more pleasure in your life? More time? More money? Different friends? More quiet time to reflect , read, study , journal or create?

_____
_____
_____
_____
_____
_____
_____
_____
_____
_____
_____

38. Under what conditions are you willing to let more pleasure into your life?

39. What do you need to put your desires into a place where they can be easily realized?

_____
_____
_____
_____
_____
_____
_____
_____

40. What are your rules about how much and what types of pleasure you permit yourself?

41. Do you honor your rules so you are in integrity with yourself?

_____
_____
_____
_____
_____
_____
_____
_____
_____
_____

42.. Do you feel you are worthy of the good?

----

43. Do you punish yourself because other people are suffering?

_____
_____
_____
_____
_____
_____
_____

44. Do you deprive yourself of pleasure thinking other people or things matters more than you ?

_____
_____
_____
_____
_____
_____
_____
_____
_____
_____

45. When you have achieved the goals you set for yourself, will you give yourself the pleasure you deserve?

_____
_____
_____
_____
_____
_____
_____
_____

46. What are the small and simple things you can do to do to incorporate pleasure into you life?

47. What appeals to you? Read good books? Meet interesting people? Expand your time helping others ? Visiting places near by that are of interest?

_____
_____
_____
_____
_____
_____
_____-

48.Name ten things you would like to do this year that are enjoyable and pleasurable.

_____
_____
_____
_____
_____
_____
_____
_____
_____

49.Do you want to explore new avenues of ease and pleasure or are you content with how things are ?

_____
_____
_____
_____
_____
____

50. Will you make the time and space for more ease and pleasure in your life? Its up to you!

_____
_____
_____
_____
_____

Meditation:

Sit comfortably with your back straight . Focus your awareness on your breathing. Breathe into your lower abdomen and fill it with your breath. Pull your breath into your chest. Slowly let the air release from your lungs. Blow away your tension. Repeat this exercise several times and begin to relax.

Bring your awareness inward. Release any tension you experience in your back, neck or jaw. Release tension in your hips, lower back , legs and feet. Feel it dissipate with every breath you take .

Release any remaining tension in your body by breathing into the areas that are tight, knotted up or congested. Feel them soften as you let your breath melt the tension. Let go. Releases tension in your lower back, behind your heart, along the sides of your body. Again, direct your breathe into these places, fill them with air and let your breath bring in healing energy .

As you ease your spirit down into your body begin to observe your negative emotions . Are you aware of your anger, fear, or sadness? Can you feel your anxiety? Do you know when you feel joyful? Sad? Angry?

Give your emotions the space to be whatever they are . Don't suppress them or stuff them down below your conscious mind. Do not get caught up in the story around them either. Simply feel your feelings . Allow them to be whatever they are.

Acknowledge them, bless them and let them dissipate back into the nothingness from which they came. Just let go . Be free . Take more deep breaths as you explore your inner being. Allow yourself to be filled up with divine love . This is the healing elixir that transforms pain into ease, anger into acceptance and fear into trust.

Emotions are real but they are not the whole picture. Don't become inflamed by them. Don't empower them or be afraid to feel them. Let go and trust the good. Feeling your feelings honors the truth of your experience.

Breathe into your chest and release the tightness , tension , or tears. The constriction longs to be released. Feel the lightness that comes with being in your truth.

Take several big breaths and let go of any ideas that continue to run through your mind. Allow the peace and pleasure of stillness and tranquility to hold you steady. This is how you release whatever emotions are stuck , unable or unwilling to be released.

Think clearly. Be at peace. Seek insight into any situation that is preventing you from experiencing pleasure and ease.

Allow your true nature to emerge as you stay calm and alert. Breathe into the stillness and surrender to your life.

Say "YES" to yourself and let life just be as it is, no matter what the conflicts are, or where the ambivalence lies. True pleasure exists in the NOW. It is not conditional on external stimulation but on your ability to be at ease and enjoy the beauty and peace of this moment.

Believe you can handle everything life gives you. Feel confident in yourself and trust the good to find you .

Feel the power of this moment. Enjoy the peace, feel the stillness . Find value in your trials. They will build your character. They will hone your being to take on higher levels of responsibility. They will teach you how to be of service to others in ways that serve the world.

Experience the pleasure of stillness and savor the peace of this moment It is a great gift in the midst of turmoil and conflict to experience this tranquility. Let it wash over you and keep you safe and steady .

Accept yourself as you are with love and grace. Feel love for yourself. Affirm your worth. Know you are worthy of claiming your good.

Be happy in this moment . Give yourself permission to experience gratitude . Enjoy the experience you have created . Take a moment to stay centered in the now.

Now take one last big breathe and smile. This is a moment to remember. Say thank you to yourself for allowing the good to flow into your heart. You are at peace, in joy and at ease.

Part Two: Chapter Six

AFFIRMATIONS:

I CAST THIS BURDEN OF LACK ON THE CHRIST WITHIN AND I GO FREE TO HAVE PLENTY.

NOTHING IS TOO GOOD FOR ME. NOTHING IS TOO WONDERFUL TO HAPPEN OR TOO GOOD TO L0SE.

I AFFIRM MY RIGHT TO HAPPINESS AND PLEASURE.

PLEASURE IS PART OF MY EVERYDAY LIFE.

I CREATIVELY TRANSFORM CHORES INTO PLEASURABLE EXPERIENCES.

I ALLOW THE GOOD INTO MY LIFE AND CLAIM ALL I WANT AND NEED FOR MYSELF.

I CLAIM HEALTH, LIMITLESS PROSPERITY, JOY, EASE AND PLEASURE. ITS OK TO ASK FOR WHAT I WANT.

I GIVE GREAT THANKS FOR THE EASE, PEACE AND PLEASURE THAT FILL MY DAY.

I RELEASE AND LET GO OF ALL THAT KEEPS ME FROM FEELING GOOD; FEAR, ANGER, GRIEF, MELT AWAY.

I TRANSFORM PAIN INTO PLEASURE THROUGH ACCEPTING MYSELF AS I AM AND AFFIRMING MY LIFE .

I RELEASE SHAME, GUILT AND MARTYRDOM RIGHT NOW. IT DOES NOT SERVE ME.

I RELEASE AND LET GO OF PAIN OR RESENTMENT THAT BLOCK ME FROM JOY AND PLEASURE .

I ENJOY PEACE, QUIET AND EASE .I LET IT FILL MY LIFE.

I AM GRATEFUL FOR THE GOOD; JOY, PLEASURE AND EASE FILL MY SPIRIT WITH DELIGHT . I RECEIVE THE GOOD NOW.

I GIVE THANKS FOR EACH AND EVERY SITUATION AND PERSON WHO HELP ME KNOW MY WORTH AND I LOVE MYSELF FULLY .

I CLAIM MY RIGHT TO THE GOOD. EASE AND PLEASURE FILL MY LIFE . I WALK IN GRACE. THANK YOU, THANK YOU, THANK YOU.

Visualization:

Imagine you have finished a project that has taken time and energy to complete. You are tired, weary and exhausted. You are happy it is done but you feel drained.

You say to yourself, "I am going to give myself the best reward for my hard work that I can imagine."

Begin to reflect what you want and need to renew your vitality, rejuvenate your spirit. Think how you can best relax and enjoy yourself before you begin your next project.

What do your days of rest look like to you? During these days you allow yourself to stay up late, eat ice cream and have special treats. You sleep late, get a massage, see an acupuncturist and call your homeopath to make an appointment.

You schedule a hair cut , get the house cleaned and your laundry taken care of. You ring a good friend, who you haven't seen in weeks ,to set up a lunch date . You need to do some shopping too.

You buy some soothing music to listen to while you soak in a hot bath filled with mineral salts and essential oils.

You discover that book you ve wanted to read and start that. You relax on the sofa and fall asleep for a long nap .

You watch a good movie and you enjoy a delicious meal. You slowly start to revive as you let go of the tension surrounding this last project.

You go to the farmer's market the next morning and to the health food store to buy fresh organic food , healthy beverages and tasty snacks to enjoy .

You start your days in prayer and meditation and bless the day for the goodness it brings you. You love starting your day being grateful and counting your blessings .

You affirm your right to enjoy the good and find pleasure in who you are and what you do. You are grateful for everything . You acknowledge the blessings all around you. You feel grace in everything.

Your body feels a need for exercise and you decide to take better care of your self. You take time for yoga stretches ; you go for a walk, have a swim , or do some physical activity to work out.

While you're walking you repeat affirmations that uplift your spirit and put you in a positive state of mind. You are willing to congratulate yourself for doing an excellent job on your project as you affirm your worth, and honor your choices for love, peace and joy.

Your spirit is full with a deep sense of gratitude and goodness. You feel blessed with love, health and joy.

When you get home from shopping you take a long, hot shower and scrub your body vigorously to wake it up with a salt rub and pungent essential oils .Your body tingles as you stimulate your circulation and removes dry skin.

You add more sensual aromatherapy oils to your body lotion and delight in the pleasure of self massage. You like taking care of yourself.

When you have finished bathing you wrap up in a comfortable robe, light incense and burn a candle. Its time for meditation . This revives your spirit and rejuvenates your energy. Each day you meditate you bring healing to your nerevous system and stimulate your brain cells. Your spirit expands and you are blessed with divine grace.

Offer a prayer for your friends and family; bless them , bless their lives and give thanks for the people you know and love. Make a forgiveness list of all the people who have hurt or wounded you and start the process of releasing them from your field.

You forgive them for who they are and release them to live their lives . You bless them and give their care over to a higher power.

You reflect on what you want to do next. You know you are too tired to make any important decisions at the moment You carefully consider the options that give you pleasure and a happy few days off.

You take time to think and reflect what you would enjoy the most. You consider a hike in nature, a dip in the sea, another massage, or just doing nothing but puttering about your place. For the moment you choose to take a rest.

After your rest you eat a wonderful meal and chat with your friend on the phone. You lay on the sofa and read your book. You fall asleep again and enjoy another pleasurable nap.

When you feel at ease you realize you want more time off for pleasure , more time to enjoy your life. You know time to relax is good for you.

You allow pleasure and rejuvenation. It opens your soul . You consider planning a holiday somewhere you have always wanted to visit.

Life begins to fall into place as you affirm your right to happiness and pleasure. You know in your heart all is well and you think about what it is that you want to do next. You become aware that life is a miracle and you are enjoying it.

Prayer:

Prayer is when we ask the Creator for what we need and long for. Here is a very simple prayer that connects you to the Holy Spirit.

Beloved Lord, I pray for peace, truth, freedom, love and joy itself. I affirm my desire for the gift of ease and pleasure without shame or guilt. I live in the truth that all good comes from you, God , including, and especially the time to rest and relax. I recognize the living spirit within me as perfect peace, absolute truth, and freedom. I am in need of renewal from time to time. Help me replenish my strength, renew my imaginative forces and see a bigger picture of what you intend for me. I ask for protection, guidance and love to sustain me in my endeavors.

I listen, I affirm, I rejoice and I welcome goodness in everything I do. I give thanks , in gratitude for all the blessings of my life. Thank you, thank you, thank you. Amen.

Blessings from the author:

Thank you for choosing to inquire what this book can offer you. It comes from the depths of my being in hopes that you feel you can allow yourself the best in life. I know we are all happier, smile more and laugh with ease when we allow the good to find us. Release what holds you down and give thanks for being able to live a life of choice, walking in grace. Be blessed with love and goodwill. Most sincerely,

Ambika Wauters, Tucson, AZ, 10/21

www.ingramcontent.com/pod-product-compliance
Lightning Source LLC
Chambersburg PA
CBHW071520080526
44588CB00011B/1499